WHO
ME?

I'm a
QUANTUM
DOT CHEMIST
now!

Who Me? series co-editors: David A. Weintraub, Professor of Astronomy, of History, and of Communication of Science and Technology, College of Arts & Science, Vanderbilt University; Ann Neely, Professor Emerita of the Practice of Education, Peabody College of Education and Human Development, Vanderbilt University; and Kevin B. Johnson, David L. Cohen University Professor of Informatics, Engineering, Pediatrics, and Communication, University of Pennsylvania. Guest editors: Bryce Emanuel, Emily Meadow, Rachael Perrotta, Anjali Raman, Carly Stewart, William Yuk. Consultants: D. Catherine Fuchs, Professor of Psychiatry and Behavioral Sciences, Department of Psychiatry & Behavioral Sciences and Pediatrics, Vanderbilt University Medical Center and Cynthia A. Rohrbeck, Associate Professor of Psychological and Brain Sciences, The George Washington University.

Published by

WS Education, an imprint of

World Scientific Publishing Co. Pte. Ltd.

5 Toh Tuck Link, Singapore 596224

USA office: 27 Warren Street, Suite 401-402, Hackensack, NJ 07601

UK office: 57 Shelton Street, Covent Garden, London WC2H 9HE

British Library Cataloguing-in-Publication Data

A catalogue record for this book is available from the British Library.

Who Me? — Vol. 6

I'M A QUANTUM DOT CHEMIST NOW!

Copyright 2023 by World Scientific Publishing Co. Pte. Ltd.

978-981-127-304-9 (hardcover)
978-981-127-305-6 (ebook for institutions)
978-981-127-306-3 (ebook for individuals)

Desk Editor: Carmen Chan

Printed in Singapore

Image credits: Sandy Rosenthal: 4, 6, 7, 8, 10 top, 12, 13, 14, 15, 16, 17, 19, 20, 24 bottom, 25, 27, 28 top, 29, 30, 31, 32 top, 33 middle, 33 bottom, 34, 35, 36, 37. **Shutterstock:** 10 bottom, 21, 22, 23, 24 top, 26, 28 bottom, 32 middle, 32 bottom. **Vanderbilt University/ Daniel Dubois:** frontispiece.

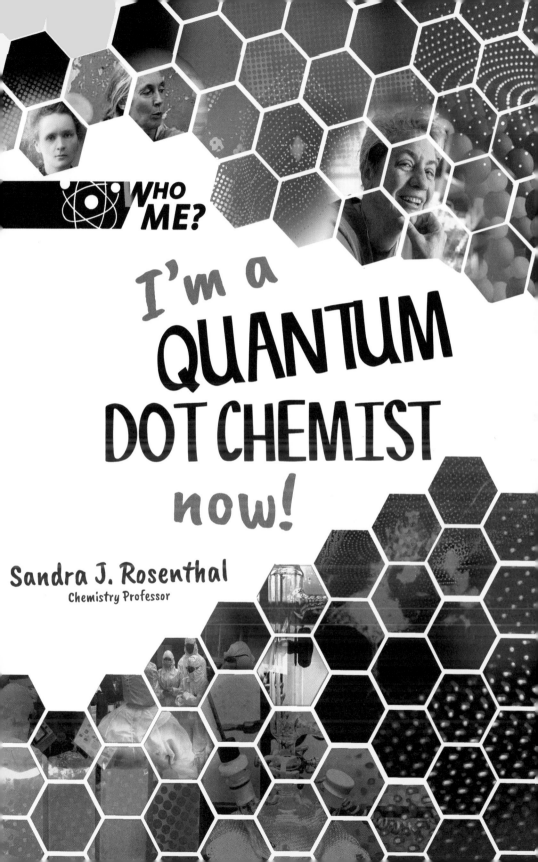

WHO
ME?

I'm a
QUANTUM
DOT CHEMIST
now!

Sandra J. Rosenthal
Chemistry Professor

Table of contents

Sandy in her lab with vials of nanocrystals that glow in different colors.

The Formula that Got Me Started

My name is Sandy. I have always loved animals. Birds, cats, dogs, horses, and even bugs. I couldn't have pets until I was grown up. Now my house is full of them.

Sandy with her dogs, James Frank (having his ears scratched) and Chewy (small; brown and white).

Sandy with her cat, Montague.

Sandy riding a horse.

Sandy holding a bird.

I spent my summers in a small town in northern Wisconsin. I was always outside and surrounded by plants and animals. Not surprisingly, I fell in love with nature. I loved thinking about how things in the world worked. Why do caterpillars have so many legs? Why do acorns become oak trees? Why do some trees lose their leaves in the winter? What other questions do you have about nature?

In second grade, I decided that I wanted to be a teacher when I grew up. Both my parents were teachers, and I wanted to be just like them! A few years later, my sixth-grade science teacher wrote something mysterious on the board. It wasn't a sentence made up of words like the one you're reading. And it wasn't a math equation, like 3 x 7 = 21. It looked sort of like a sentence and sort of like an equation at the same time. My teacher said it was a *chemical formula*. "What is that?" I wondered. She told us that the letters, symbols, and numbers in the formula are part of the language used in chemistry. Chemistry is a type of science. Chemists study the things that make up the world. A chemist does experiments to better understand these things.

We learned that scientists discovered how plants make food. This formula is like a recipe for how they do that. The process is called photosynthesis. Chemists figured out how to write down this formula to explain to others how this process works.

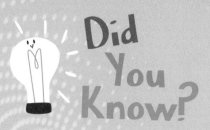

Did You Know?

Photosynthesis

$$6CO_2 + 6H_2O \rightarrow C_6H_{12}O_6 + 6O_2$$

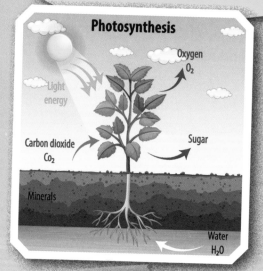

Photosynthesis

Light energy

Oxygen O_2

Carbon dioxide Co_2

Sugar

Minerals

Water H_2O

Plants combine sunlight with water from the soil and carbon dioxide from the air to make sugar and oxygen. This process is called photosynthesis. The sugar is stored in the leaves. The oxygen is released into the atmosphere.

In this chemical formula, the letters represent elements. Elements are different kinds of atoms. Atoms are particles that are so small we cannot see them with just our eyes. Everything in the world is made of atoms. Even you are! So are roads, cars, phones, and the air. The H in the formula represents the element called hydrogen. O represents the element oxygen. Those are just two examples of elements. Nitrogen, gold, silver, and mercury are also elements. Can you name some other elements?

When elements interact, they can combine to make molecules. Chemists use a special code for molecules. H_2O represents a molecule made of two hydrogen atoms and one oxygen atom. That's the formula for water! CO_2 represents a molecule made of one carbon atom and two oxygen atoms. That's the formula for carbon dioxide!

Look at the big formula written on page 10. Six molecules of carbon dioxide are added to six molecules of water. The plus sign means that the molecules interact. When they interact, the atoms in the molecules can separate from each other and recombine in different ways.

The arrow represents time. It tells us that a reaction happened. The molecules on the left side of the arrow combined into new molecules. The new molecules are written on the right side of the arrow. The first molecule on the right side is sugar. The second one is oxygen.

That formula describes a chemical process called photosynthesis. When plants do this, they use sunlight to power a chemical reaction. That reaction combines water and carbon dioxide to make sugar and the oxygen we breathe. So cool!

Here's another chemical formula. Can you figure out what it means?

$$2H_2 + O_2 \rightarrow 2H_2O$$

After learning about the chemical formula for photosynthesis, I was hooked. I felt like dancing. At home that day, all I could think of was how beautiful and magical that formula was. But the formula wasn't magic, it was science! And it was in a powerful new language I wanted to understand. That day in school changed my life. I still wanted to be a teacher, but now I wanted to be a science teacher, probably a high school chemistry teacher. I wanted to teach other people about this new language I hadn't even learned yet. I also hadn't been to high school yet. In fact, I was only in my first year of middle school. But now I had a plan!

Sandy, age 5, and her older brother Rob, age 6.

Sandy playing third base on her high school softball team.

The Buffalo Grove High School basketball team. Sandy is in the back row, standing next to Coach Dineen.

Science wasn't the only thing I was interested in when I was younger. I had an older brother, Rob. He let me tag along with him to play baseball, basketball, football, and softball with his friends. I also played on my high school basketball and softball teams. To train for sports, you have to be hardworking and manage your time well. That way, you have enough time for school, homework, sports practices, meals, and time with friends. Plus, if your grades are not good enough, you don't get to play on the team! I think playing on sports teams made me a good student. Sometimes, I even did my homework while riding the bus to games. By the time I got to college, I knew how to plan my days to get everything done. That helped me be a good college student.

2 Discovering and Living with Bipolar Disorder

After high school, I decided to go to Valparaiso University in Indiana. I played on their basketball team. I also studied chemistry. My plan changed a bit because I loved sports so much. Now, my goal was to become a high school chemistry teacher and a basketball coach.

Sandy in college with her friends.

Sandy playing basketball for Valparaiso University.

During my first year in college, I took a chemistry class. We did an experiment about electricity. I was excited to do this experiment. When I was done, I wrote a lab report that described what I learned. I thought I had done the experiment very carefully. But my professor, Dr. Kosman, gave me a low grade. He said my answer was unexpected. Maybe I used a piece of equipment incorrectly, he said. This puzzled me. I was sure I had done the lab work correctly! I asked to repeat the experiment. When I did, I got the same result. I now had my first research question:

Why was the experiment not working?

Dr. Kosman came in on a Saturday so I could redo the experiment. I repeated the experiment exactly and got the same result. Now we were both curious. He taught me how to use the library to do research on chemistry. I read about experiments that professional scientists did. I discovered that somebody, way back in 1939, had done the same experiment. Based on what we learned, we changed how we made our measurements.

Finally, I got the expected result. I also got a great grade for my work! I learned something else that day too. I realized that I love doing research and discovering new things.

Valparaiso University presented me with this Distinguished Student Award when I graduated!

Dr. Kosman suggested I consider teaching chemistry in college instead of in high school. As a college professor, I could teach and do research. That combination sounded perfect to me. To do this, I would have to go to graduate school after college. He told me I needed to earn a degree called a PhD. People who study for PhD degrees learn how to do research.

Soon, I was taking classes in chemistry, math, and physics. These subjects all prepared me for graduate school.

Sandy in her commencement gown after graduating from college. She is standing next to Dr. Kosman.

I was always the only girl on the court when I played basketball with my brother and his friends. I was often the only girl in the classroom in my college science classes. And I only had one female professor for a class. Playing basketball with my brother and his friends prepared me well for these experiences. I might have been the only girl, but I was never intimidated. I knew I was as tough and smart as everybody else in the room. I wanted to show everyone that women can be scientists too. I was going to be a professor!

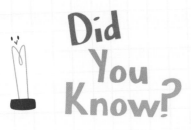

Did You Know?

The Physics of Bouncing a Basketball

Have you ever bounced a basketball? If you drop it from eye level, how high do you think it will bounce? What if you dropped it from waist level?

You may have noticed that the ball always bounces back up almost as high as from where it was dropped. This means that the amount of energy in the basketball is almost the same after the bounce as it was before you dropped it. The basketball does lose a little bit of energy, though. When it hits the floor, a little bit of energy is transferred from the basketball to the floor. That energy heats up the floor, just a tiny bit! That transfer of energy from the basketball to the floor is called friction. Basketball courts for professional players are made so well that the basketballs lose almost no energy when they bounce.

Try dropping different kinds of balls. Try dropping balls on different kinds of floors. Which balls keep the most energy? Which floors take away the most energy from the bouncing balls?

Something else important happened to me in college. I met my future husband in a physics class during our first year of college!

Sandy and her husband Adam on their wedding day!

Our daughter, Jaimie, is now 18 years old. She is almost ready for college!

Jaimie, at 10 years old, opening a present while her stuffed dolphin, Finn, watches.

Sandy's daughter, Jaimie, plays basketball, just like her mom!

Jaimie also loves mountain biking.

After graduating from college, I started graduate school. I went to the University of Chicago. That's where I learned to be a chemist. I earned my PhD working with the distinguished scientist, Graham Fleming. For my research project, I used a kind of light called a laser to study how liquids move. A laser emits a beam of light, just like a flashlight. But lasers do not have light bulbs. They produce light in a different way. And the light from this laser turns on and off and on and off, more than a million times every billionth of a second! That's a quadrillion— or 1,000,000,000,000,000—times every second! When I was almost done with my research project, I became interested in something very cool called quantum dots. I'll tell you more about them in the next chapter!

I loved living in Chicago. I enjoyed riding my bicycle along the shore of Lake Michigan. In the summers, I also had fun playing softball with my friends. And I loved the tall skyscrapers and the pizza!

Chicago is famous for deep-dish pizza. Yum!

Six weeks after finishing graduate school, I got very ill. I did not sleep for a whole week. It was like being sick, but I never had a cough or a sniffle. At that time, my doctors and I didn't know what was wrong. It took six months for me to feel better. Once I was healthy again, I moved to California to work as a scientist doing chemistry experiments. My goal was the same. I wanted to become a chemistry professor. Two years later, I became ill again. I became so agitated and distressed that I could not sleep. But after four months, I got better again. Then I moved to Nashville, Tennessee. There, I started my dream job. I was a chemistry professor at Vanderbilt University.

Four years after the first time I got sick, I became ill again. During the spring and summer, I felt like I was on top of the world! I was happy and full of energy. During the fall and winter, I felt extra sad and was always tired. I was also always worried. When the season changed from winter to spring, I started to feel better. But by the next winter, I got sad and tired again.

This cartoon illustrates how my emotions go up and down with the seasons.

Five years after the first time I got sick, my doctors determined that I have **bipolar disorder**. Two years later, I learned that I have seasonal bipolar disorder. This is a common form of bipolar disorder. People like me go through waves of emotion. My highs are higher than for most people. And they last longer. Also, my lows are lower and last longer than for most people. It can be scary. It is like being on a roller coaster without a seat belt. I am grateful that I had help from Dr. Kay Jamison, who is an international expert on bipolar disorder.

People with bipolar disorder struggle to control their feelings. We can get angrier or more irritated than most people do. We also struggle to control our energy levels. Sometimes it can feel like we have way too much energy. Other times, we feel like we have none at all. Sometimes we can feel way too happy and end up not taking good care of ourselves, like not getting enough sleep. Sometimes we can feel way too sad and depressed for a long time. But, it is different for everyone. I feel sad in the winter and happy in the summer. Other people with bipolar disorder may feel sad or happy at different times of the year. It is called bipolar disorder because my energy and emotions bounce back and forth. They go from one extreme to the other. It is like going from the North Pole to the South Pole and back again.

The doctors gave me medicine to help me. It worked and still does. The medicine is important for my brain health.

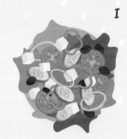

I always have to remember to take it the way my doctors instructed. I also have to get enough sleep and exercise. And I need to eat healthy food. I still lose energy and get depressed from August until late February.

Then, I start feeling better. My favorite months of the year are March, April, and May. This can be a very creative time. I feel like I am looking at the 500 pieces of a jigsaw puzzle and I know exactly where each piece

fits. But then the energy becomes too much. I'm like Iron Man with an arc reactor in my chest, and when I am trying to sleep, that arc reactor is burning a hole in the ceiling, burning a hole through the roof, and spraying my energy through the universe. I struggle to control all of that energy. Then August rolls around again. But with my medicine, my mood swings are smaller and under control. And I can still teach my students, do chemistry research, and raise my daughter.

Jaimie is ready for college now.

One of the things that is hard about **depression** is that at the end of the day, you play your day over and over again in your head. Did I make someone angry? Did I misunderstand something that was said to me? Did someone misunderstand me? Did I do something wrong? These feelings have a big word to describe them. That word is *rumination*. One of the worst parts of depression is rumination. I always wonder if I have done something wrong.

You can't catch bipolar disorder. It is not like the flu or a cold. It is not caused by bacteria or a virus. But it is something that can be **inherited** from a parent or grandparent.

The cool thing about my family is that they chose me. I'm adopted! This made me wonder where my bipolar disorder came from. I found out that my biological father had undiagnosed bipolar disorder. I inherited my brain-based disorder from him.

3 Quantum Dots

I do research in my lab about **quantum dots**. Sounds cool, right? It is! You will need to know two things about quantum dots. Then I'll tell you what I learned about them.

First, quantum dots are nanoparticles. That means they are made of just a few hundred atoms. If you measured how big they are, you'd find they are just a few nanometers across. That means they are incredibly small. They are too small to see, even with a magnifying glass. But we can see them with a very special kind of microscope called an electron microscope.

Each vial contains a small amount of quantum dots. They are dissolved in a liquid (like dissolving sugar in water). The liquid is called toluene. Scientists can modify the quantum dots so that they dissolve in the liquid. Otherwise, they would sink to the bottom. The smallest quantum dots give off white light. The ones that give off blue light are a little bigger. The ones that give off green light are even bigger, and the ones that give off red light are the biggest.

Did You Know?

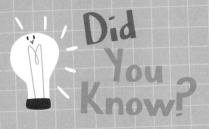

What is a Nanometer? What is a Billionth?

A billion is a big number. How big? Imagine that you work at a gas station pumping gas in cars. You put 10 gallons of gas into the tank of one car. Then you do that for another car. You repeat this every 10 minutes. How many cars did you put gas into in one hour? Pretty soon you'll be tired!

You do that without stopping for every hour of the day (all 24 hours!). You don't go home and go to sleep. Instead, you do this again tomorrow. And the next day. And 365 days in a row for a whole year and 366 days in leap years. And you keep doing this, without resting, for 2,000 years. Altogether, you would have pumped 1 billion gallons of gas.

Can you think of other ways to do something that adds up to 1 billion?

A nanometer is a very small distance. Other words that are used to measure distances are inches, feet, and miles in

A human hair seen magnified in a microscope.

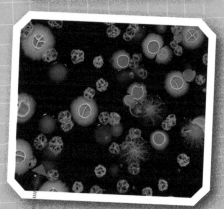

Many bacteria seen magnified in a microscope.

the United States and millimeters, meters, and kilometers in other parts of the world. An inch is one-twelfth of a foot. So you need 12 inches to make one foot. A millimeter is one-thousandth of a meter. That means you need one thousand millimeters to make one meter. A nanometer is one billionth of a meter. That means you need one billion nanometers to make one meter. Do you know how many meters you need to make one kilometer? Do you know how many feet you need to make one mile?

The width of a strand of human hair is very small. But that width is about 75,000 nanometers! A bacterium is only a few thousand nanometers wide. Imagine slicing a bacterium into a thousand tiny slices. Each piece would be about one nanometer wide.

Use this scale to measure the size of your hand in nanometers. What's your answer? Measure the sizes of some other objects. What are their sizes, in nanometers?

How Big is Your Hand?

centimeters	
	200 million nanometers
19	190 million nanometers
18	180 million nanometers
17	170 million nanometers
16	160 million nanometers
15	150 million nanometers
14	140 million nanometers
13	130 million nanometers
12	120 million nanometers
11	110 million nanometers
10	100 million nanometers
9	90 million nanometers
8	80 million nanometers
7	70 million nanometers
6	60 million nanometers
5	50 million nanometers
4	40 million nanometers
3	30 million nanometers
2	20 million nanometers
1	10 million nanometers
	0 nanometers

Scientists who study small things like bacteria and atoms use special kinds of tools. Nanotechnology is the word we use for the tools and machines that can pick up or measure or take pictures of nanometer-sized objects. Nanotechnology can be used in many different ways! Nanotechnology is used to make computer chips that are only 10 nanometers thick. Nanotechnology is also used to make glues stickier in hotter temperatures and to design better sunscreens. How do you think nanotechnology might be used to solve some of the world's biggest problems? Nanometer, nanoparticle, and nanotechnology all begin with the prefix nano. What do you think nano means?

This is a transmission electron microscope. It is an important piece of nanotechnology. It sends a beam of tiny particles toward the tiny object we want to study. The tiny particles are called electrons. Some electrons bounce off of the object. Others go right through it! Scientists use information collected from all of those electrons to make pictures of the object.

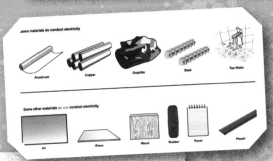

The objects in the top row are conductors. The objects in the bottom row are insulators.

Second, quantum dots are made of a special kind of material called a semiconductor. Semiconductors are in-between conductors and insulators. Conductors allow electricity to travel through them. Metals like copper or iron are conductors. Insulators block electricity. Insulators can be made from clay or plastic. Scientists can control semiconductors to make them conductors or insulators.

We make quantum dots in my lab. To make quantum dots, we use special tools to put together atoms from two different elements. The elements we use are cadmium and selenium. We also use the tools to design the quantum dots to have special shapes and sizes.

To make a quantum dot, we use this glass bottle with three openings. It is called a three-neck flask. We insert a molecule that has cadmium into the bottle. Then we add a molecule that has selenium in it. We heat the bottle to a temperature that is much higher than the boiling point of water. The three necks control the temperature and keep the fluid inside the flask. Once the mixture is super hot, the cadmium and selenium atoms join together to make super small crystals. This process is called nucleation! We then lower the temperature. At the low temperature, more atoms slowly collect onto the nanocrystals. This makes the nanocrystals grow bigger without making new, small crystals. Nucleation is the same process that makes bubbles grow in a glass of soda. You could pour soda into a glass and watch that happen!

This is what a cadmium-selenide quantum dot would look like if it were big enough to see. The big red dots are selenium atoms. The small green dots are cadmium atoms.

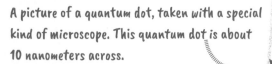

A picture of a quantum dot, taken with a special kind of microscope. This quantum dot is about 10 nanometers across.

3 nm

If you shine a light on a quantum dot, it will glow! The smallest quantum dots glow blue or even violet. Bigger ones glow orange or even red.

4 Cleanrooms and Classrooms

We study our quantum dots in a special room called a cleanroom. A cleanroom is a room that scientists try to keep super clean. There is no dust or dirt on the floor or in the air. No stray hairs or flying bugs. A cleanroom has machines that control the air temperature. Other machines prevent air from flowing into or out of the room. And other machines filter the air to remove dust and other tiny particles.

Having a cleanroom is important when you work with nanotechnology. The nanoparticles are so small that even dust can contaminate them. This means that dust can make the room dirty and unusable.

Scientists working in cleanrooms wear special clothes, including gloves, goggles, and masks.

These scientists are working in the cleanroom, using nanomaterials to make bigger things. The equipment in the cleanroom can make patterns in nanomaterials. These scientists are making a device that will make light go around things. That will make these other things invisible!

Scientists working in cleanrooms can contaminate the room. The cleanroom has to be protected from the oil on their skin, the hair on their heads, and the dirt on their shoes. If they coughed or sneezed, they would contaminate the cleanroom. This means that people who enter cleanrooms must wear special clothes. Their suits cover their whole bodies. Cleanrooms can even have sticky floors. Then the dirt particles on shoes come off on the floor instead of on the equipment.

I wanted to use the cleanroom to make solar cells with our quantum dots. Solar cells absorb sunlight and turn the sunlight into electricity. A quantum dot that did that could make better, less expensive solar cells.

Did You Know?

VINSE

At Vanderbilt, I was the director of VINSE for 12 years. VINSE is the Vanderbilt Institute of Nanoscale Science and Engineering. One of my biggest accomplishments as director was that I built a cleanroom. Well, I didn't do the construction work myself. But I designed it and made sure it was built the right way. It took me nearly five years to get this done. Now, lots of scientists can do research in the cleanroom.

These students are the Tech Crew, all wearing their cleanroom suits.

High school students come on field trips to work in the cleanroom. They have made solar cells using blackberry juice and paint pigment! Vanderbilt students learn how to operate and maintain the cleanroom. We call them the Tech Crew. Tech Crew members help professors do new experiments in the cleanroom.

A group of high school students on a field trip to the cleanroom.

I did not succeed in making a solar cell. I was disappointed. But I did something else that was incredible. When we tried to make a solar cell, we squeezed our quantum dots into a special shape. When we did that, they emitted white light. That means that our quantum dots emitted purple, blue, green, yellow, orange, and red light all at the same time. Nobody had ever done that before! Someday, our special quantum dots may be used to make white-light LEDs. LED means *light emitting diode*. That's a light bulb that uses very little energy.

A small vial of cadmium-selenide quantum dots emitting white light.

Did You Know?

White Light, Prisms, and Rainbows

White light is made up of every color of light. Light from the Sun is white light. When white light goes through a piece of glass with the right shape, called a prism, the white light separates into an entire rainbow of colors. Water droplets in the air act like prisms to create rainbows.

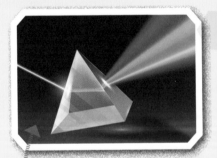

White light enters the prism and comes out as a rainbow of colors.

A rainbow.

You can do your own experiment to make a rainbow of colors. You need a flashlight, a clear glass full of water, and a small, flat mirror. Put the mirror in the glass of water. In a dark room, shine the flashlight through the side of the glass at the mirror. What do you see?

Suddenly, I was on the news. Newspapers, magazines, and television had stories about me. The magazine *Popular Mechanics* awarded me their Breakthrough Award. The American Chemical Society awarded me with a medal made of solid gold!

Sandy's award from *Popular Mechanics*.

Now, we are doing a new experiment with my quantum dots. We are studying two chemicals that are active in our brains. The chemicals are *serotonin* and *dopamine*. They are called *neurotransmitters*.

Sandy won this award in 2018. It is given out by the American Chemical Society to chemists who have made significant contributions to our understanding of chemistry and have served society in important ways.

Our brains have neurons. Neurons are special nerve cells that send messages to other neurons or muscles. Those messages do things like make our muscles move, our hearts beat, our lungs take in air, and our brains work. But the neurons need help.

Think of the neurons as if they were members of a relay team running a race. The first runner starts, holding a baton in her hand. That runner runs 100 meters down the track. She then has to hand the baton to the next runner before that runner takes her turn. Together, the team of runners transports the baton to where it needs to go—the finish line. Neurotransmitters are like batons. Without them, information cannot travel in our brains from one nerve to another nerve or to a muscle fiber.

Dopamine and serotonin are important in brain health. Both may play roles in the problem of bipolar disorder. I am using quantum dots to try to learn what these molecules do in the brain. We attach quantum dots to the neurotransmitters. This process is like putting tags on clothes. We then use special lights to make the quantum dots glow. That way, we can watch where the drugs are going inside the brain.

We can't do this in a human brain yet. But we can do this in slices taken from mouse brains. We can also do this with neurons that we grow in special containers called Petri dishes. With these experiments, we hope to learn how to help people with brain health problems like bipolar disorder.

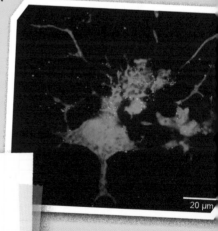

20 µm

The bright orange spots are where the quantum dots are glowing.

Sandy teaching General Chemistry to first-year students at Vanderbilt University.

Teaching has always been my dream. I feel very lucky to be a chemistry professor. I love teaching chemistry to my students. I also want my students to be happy and healthy. So I also teach them about the importance of brain health. I talk about how I have struggled with bipolar disorder and the importance of getting help from my doctors. I want them to know that they can be successful even if they struggle with big changes in their mood and energy that last a long time.

I also teach them healthy habits for learning and life. They need a full night of sleep, good food, and exercise every day. So do you! These healthy habits keep both their brains and bodies healthy.

I also teach a class about brain health. I teach my students that everyone worries sometimes. That's normal. But some people have anxiety. They can't control their nervousness, and they worry all the time. Also, everyone feels sad or depressed sometimes. That's normal. But some people have depression. That means that they feel very sad and have low energy almost all the time. We can help take care of ourselves and our friends by learning about these conditions. And doctors and therapists can help people with anxiety or depression, just like they helped me with bipolar disorder.

I was very lucky to grow up knowing I wanted to learn about science. Now, I want every middle school student to do science experiments. That's how they can discover if they like science.

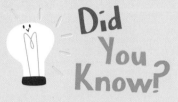

Did You Know?

Science at Home

I work with middle school teachers in Tennessee to help them add science experiments to their classes. We made kits so that every student had the materials for the cool experiments. I think that everyone should do hands-on experiments. They are so much fun!

See if you can do this experiment. It is called *depositing a thin film of material*. This is just like what we do in the cleanroom. Later, use the link at the end of the book to find more experiments you can do!

These are the things you need to do this experiment:
- A strip of black construction paper
- A small jar of clear nail polish
- A shallow dish, like a pie pan

Next, follow these steps:

1. Fill the dish with water
2. Slide the construction paper into the water
3. Add two drops of nail polish to the dish of water
4. Wait two minutes
5. Remove the construction paper from the water and drain off all the fluid

There is now a thin film on the construction paper. Can you see it? Hold the paper up so that light reflects off the paper. How many colors can you see? The nail polish is clear, so where did these colors come from? Do you think this would work with colored nail polish? Where have you seen this same kind of thing happen in nature?

I get to teach, do research, and, most importantly, help students and my community. Helping others is important to me because I want to inspire others to become scientists. Teaching others what I know is very rewarding! You can do this too!

GLOSSARY

Atoms   The smallest pieces of ordinary matter. More than 100 different kinds of atoms exist.

Bipolar disorder   An illness that causes a person to sometimes go through extreme changes in mood and behavior.

Chemistry   The science that deals with the properties, composition, and structure of molecules, how they interact, and how they absorb and release energy.

Cleanroom   A specially built room made to keep out dust, pollen, and other airborne particles that is used by scientists and engineers for doing experiments.

Depression   An illness, also known as a serious mood disorder, that continues for many days or weeks, during which a person may feel sad or anxious or hopeless and may lose interest in regular activities like eating or working.

Element   One of the 118 known kinds of atoms.

Inherit

To receive a trait, like brown hair or bipolar disorder, from a parent.

Molecule

A small piece of matter made from a combination of two or more atoms.

Nanotechnology

The tools and machines that can pick up or measure or take pictures of nanometer-sized objects.

Neurotransmitter

A chemical active in our brains that helps neurons transmit signals from one neuron to the next and to our muscles.

Photosynthesis

A chemical process plants use to combine sunlight, water, and carbon dioxide to make sugar and oxygen.

Quantum dots

Small particles made of just a few hundred atoms that can absorb and re-emit light.

Solar cell

A device that collects sunlight and converts it into electricity.

Discussion Questions

1. In addition to playing on a sports team, what other kinds of activities could you participate in that would help you learn to manage your time and your health?

2. Do you know anyone in your family who has a brain health problem like anxiety, depression, or bipolar disorder? What do they do to manage their brain health?

3. Can you think of ways to keep dust and pollen and other airborne particles out of a cleanroom? Why do you think scientists need cleanrooms?

4. What kinds of ideas do you have for making nanoparticles? What would your nanoparticles do?

Additional Resources

1. Sandy's home page:

2. Size, scale, and measurement activities:

3. Sandy talks about how bipolar disorder has affected her research:

4. More experiments you can do at home, from Vanderbilt Students Volunteer for Science:

5. Bipolar Bear by Victoria M. Remmel:

6. Bipolar disorder information for children:

7. Bipolar disorder information for teenagers:

8. Mental Health Resources for Young Adults with Bipolar Disorder: